BLACK EXCELLENCE AFFIRMATIONS FOR MEN

POSITIVE AFFIRMATIONS FOR KINGS TO INCREASE PEACE, HEALTH, POWER, WEALTH, CONFIDENCE, SUCCESS, FOCUS, LOVE, AND SEX!

TASHA TINSLEY

information contained within this document, including, but not limited to, — errors, omissions, or inaccuracies.

CONTENTS

INTRODUCTION

Affirmations can hold immense significance for black men as they offer a powerful tool for self-reclamation, self-empowerment, and cultivating a positive self-image. Amidst stereotypes, systemic inequalities, and pervasive prejudices, affirmations stand as a beacon of strength, guiding black men towards re-establishing their self-esteem and realizing their inherent potential.

By reading, repeating, and listening to affirmations, black men can transform the narrative surrounding black masculinity. Black men reaffirm their worth, capabilities, and virtues by enveloping themselves in positive messages. This practice allows them to break free from the damaging narratives and stereotypes that often attempt to confine them to limited, prejudiced perceptions.

The power of affirmations lies in their ability to penetrate deep into the subconscious, restructuring beliefs and thoughts. When black men repeatedly speak or absorb positive affirmations, they nurture a mindset of strength, resilience, and self-belief. This practice becomes a mechanism to counteract the insidious impact of societal pressures, racial biases, and stereotypes that can otherwise chip away at one's self-esteem.

Affirmations act as a mirror, reflecting every black man's inherent dignity, strength, and potential. By surrounding themselves with positive messages, they create a shield against the negativity that seeks to diminish their sense of self-worth. This reclamation of self-esteem becomes a foundational pillar upon which they can build their lives with confidence and purpose.

Furthermore, affirmations become a means of defiance—a tool that allows black men to break free from societal constraints, embracing their individuality, strengths, and uniqueness. Moreover, affirmations foster a sense of personal power—a recognition of their innate ability to shape their destinies. This newfound sense of personal power enables them to navigate challenges with resilience and grace, empowering them to stand tall amidst adversity.

Embracing positive affirmations isn't just about fostering self-esteem; it's about reclaiming the throne of their lives. It's about stepping into their inherent greatness, recognizing themselves as kings in their own right—noble, powerful, and capable of shaping their destinies. Through affirmations, black men can reclaim their narrative, fortify their self-esteem, and step into the fullness of their potential as the kings they were meant to be.

CHAPTER 1
AFFIRMATIONS FOR STARTING THE DAY RIGHT

- I will learn simple and complex topics.
- I will make today a great day.
- My body is strong, and my mind is well-rested.
- I will take care of my health and my spirit first today.
- I will accomplish amazing things today.
- I am capable of achieving anything I set my mind to.
- Today is a new opportunity to embrace all my strengths.
- I emit confidence and attract success.
- My goals are within reach, and I am taking steps to achieve them.

- I am a powerful force for positivity in the world.
- I am grateful for the gift of a new day and the possibilities it brings.
- I'm confident in my ability to make the right decisions for myself.
- Positive energy and good vibes surround me.
- I am a beacon of positivity and inspire others around me.
- My mind is eager for the challenges ahead.
- My mind is focused on the challenges ahead.
- My mind is clear for the challenges ahead.
- I am deserving of success and happiness.
- I choose to let go of negativity.
- I will start my day off right.
- I am constantly growing.
- I am constantly evolving into the best version of myself.
- I am confident in my abilities.
- I attract abundance and prosperity into my life.
- Today, I choose peace in every situation.
- Today, I choose love.
- I am grateful for my health and vitality.

- I am open to new opportunities and welcome positive change.
- I am welcome to positive change.
- I am a leader with compassion and drive.
- I lead with strength and integrity.
- I am a leader, and I lead with compassion.
- I am proud of the person I am becoming.
- Right now, I will make choices that align with my goals and values.
- I am a beacon of light, spreading positivity wherever I go.
- I am a draw for success, and I attract opportunities effortlessly.
- I am at peace with my past, present, and future.
- I am a loving and supportive friend, partner, and family member.
- I am resilient, and I bounce back from challenges with grace.
- My life is filled with purpose, passion, and fulfillment.
- I am enough for all the good that life has to offer.
- I trust the journey and the process.
- I am grateful for the lessons of yesterday and the blessings of today.

- I approach each day with a positive attitude.
- I am constantly growing and improving.
- I represent strength for those around me.
- I am confident in my ability to make intelligent decisions.
- Now, I choose happiness and to let go of worry and stress.
- I am a valuable and unique individual worthy of love and respect.
- I am excited about the possibilities of today.

CHAPTER 2

AFFIRMATIONS FOR UNSHAKABLE CONFIDENCE

- I will have unshakable confidence today and onwards.
- My self-assurance grows stronger with each challenge I face.
- I emit confidence.
- I emit charisma.
- I have a positive attitude.
- I trust my instincts and make decisions with confidence.
- I am a powerful and capable individual.
- Confidence is my second nature.
- I handle any situation with ease.
- I am secure in who I am.
- I am secure in what I bring to the table
- My past does not define me.

- My resilience and growth shape me.
- Challenges are opportunities for me to showcase my capabilities.
- My confidence inspires those around me.
- I can and will overcome any obstacles in my path.
- I am a draw for success.
- My confidence is unshakable.
- My resilience and growth shape me.
- I face uncertainty with courage and unwavering confidence.
- I am unwavering in my convictions.
- I embrace the unknown with confidence and curiosity.
- I am bold.
- I am fearless.
- I am capable of achieving greatness.
- My confidence uplifts those around me.
- My confidence inspires those around me.
- I am ready to embrace the limitless possibilities before me.
- I trust my journey.
- I am a force to be reckoned with.
- My confidence is unyielding.
- My confidence empowers me to embrace new experiences.

- My confidence empowers me to take risks.
- I trust my decisions and stand firm in my beliefs.
- I exude confidence in every aspect of my life.
- There are no problems when I'm the equation.
- I trust that the universe is working in my favor.
- I am the architect of my destiny, and I build it with confidence.
- Confidence is mine to own, and I claim it with pride.
- I am a confident, capable, and resilient man.
- I trust myself to handle any situation with grace and poise.
- I emit self-assurance, and people are drawn to my confidence.
- I am confident in my uniqueness and embrace my individuality.
- I am unafraid to pursue my dreams.
- I am confident in my ability to create positive change.
- I am always guided toward greater and greater success.

- I confidently pursue my goals with determination and focus.
- I have the strength to overcome any adversity.
- Confidence is my ally.
- I am confident and ready.

CHAPTER 3

AFFIRMATIONS FOR VIBRANT HEALTH AND WELLNESS

- My body is a temple.
- I treat my body with love and respect.
- I am grateful for good health.
- I nourish my body with wholesome foods.
- I am in tune with my body's needs.
- Each day, I am getting more energetic.
- Daily, I am getting healthier.
- I am at peace with myself.
- Today, I am getting stronger.
- I am at peace with my past, present, and future.
- I am promoting overall total prosperity.
- I am grateful for the healing power that resides within me.

- My mind, body, and spirit are in perfect harmony.
- I emit good health from my life choices.
- I attract wellness into my life.
- I am grateful for this abundance of energy.
- My body is capable of healing and renewal.
- My body is a resilient vessel.
- I am mindful of my breath and health.
- I listen to my body's signals and respond accordingly.
- I am a draw for total prosperity.
- I am the architect of my health, and I build it with good choices.
- I am surrounded by a vibrant environment that promotes wellness.
- I release any negativity from my life.
- I am grateful for the opportunity to take care of my physical health.
- Each day, my body becomes stronger.
- Daily, my body becomes healthier.
- Every single day, my body becomes more vibrant.
- I approach exercise with joy, knowing it contributes to my total prosperity.
- My immune system is robust.
- I am a vessel of positive energy.

- I am a vessel of radiating health.
- I am a vessel of vitality.
- I invite relaxation and peace.
- I am in control of my health.
- I am resilient to illness.
- I make choices that benefit me.
- I am grateful for the power of a good night's sleep.
- I am surrounded by a circle of support that uplifts me.
- I am committed to living a healthy life.
- I radiate wellness to those around me.
- I am too vibrant to be brought down.
- I am grateful for the ability to heal.
- I am grateful for the wisdom of my body.
- I am grateful for the resilience of my spirit.
- I am at peace with my body.
- I am grateful for the resilience of my mind.
- I am grateful for the abundance of fresh air that nourishes my body.
- I am surrounded by healing energy.
- I am surrounded by love.

CHAPTER 4

AFFIRMATIONS FOR UNLEASHING INNER POWER

- My inner power is unstoppable.
- My inner power is a source of strength.
- My inner power is a source of resilience.
- I am a force to be reckoned with.
- My inner power is a source of courage.
- I am a powerhouse of energy.
- I am a powerhouse of vitality.
- I am a powerhouse of inner strength.
- I am a draw for positive energy.
- I embrace my inner power with confidence.
- The immense power within me moves me.
- I am a channel for the universe's energy.
- My inner power is boundless.
- I trust that my inner power is more than enough to conquer any obstacles.

- I am a warrior!
- My inner power is a well of creativity.
- My inner power swells with inspiration.
- I am a vessel of immense power.
- My inner power is a pool of resilience.
- My inner power is a driving force.
- I am a beacon of inner power.
- I am a beacon of radiating strength.
- I am a beacon of confidence.
- I'm capable of achieving greatness.
- My inner power is a catalyst for positive change in my life.
- I will not be limited by external circumstances.
- My inner power transcends my limits.
- My inner power empowers me to overcome challenges.
- I am a vessel of absolute energy.
- I am a fierce advocate for my dreams.
- The fire of my inner power fuels me.
- My inner power helps me bounce back from any setback.
- My inner power is a reservoir of determination.
- I release any self-imposed limitations.
- I am a target for opportunities.

- My inner power is a force for good.
- I am a vessel of strength in all endeavors.
- I wield my inner power with wisdom and grace.
- I trust my inner power.
- I am a warrior of light.
- My inner power is ready to be unleashed at any moment.
- I am a vessel of empowerment.
- I am aligned with the universal flow of energy.
- My inner power is in harmony with the universe.
- I have transformative power.
- My inner power guides me through challenges.
- I trust the process of unleashing my inner power when necessary.
- I am a conduit for divine energy.
- My inner power is a gift from the universe.
- I am grateful for my inner power that empowers me in my life.

CHAPTER 5

AFFIRMATIONS FOR ABUNDANT WEALTH AND PROSPERITY

- I am a draw for abundance and attract prosperity effortlessly.
- Wealth and prosperity flow to me in unexpected and joyful ways.
- I am worthy of unlimited financial success and abundance.
- Every day, I am moving closer to financial freedom.
- I am grateful for the abundance surrounding me in all aspects of life.
- I attract wealth with every positive thought and action I take.
- Abundance is my right, and I claim it with gratitude.

- I am open to receiving prosperity from multiple sources.
- I am a money draw, and my income is constantly increasing.
- I believe in my ability to create wealth and success.
- My mind is a powerful tool for attracting unlimited prosperity.
- I feel the energy of abundance that flows through me.
- I am grateful for the wealth that is pouring into my life.
- The universe conspires to bring me prosperity and success.
- I am in control of my financial destiny.
- My actions create constant prosperity.
- I am blessed.
- I am open to receiving the abundance that the universe has for me.
- Money flows to me quickly and effortlessly.
- I am a rich source of ideas.
- I am worthy of all the prosperity that life has to offer.
- I am worthy of all the success that life has to offer.
- My creativity brings financial abundance

- I am worthy of all the abundance that life has to offer.
- I am open to receiving all the wealth the universe has for me.
- I am in harmony with the energy of money.
- I am surrounded by abundance.
- I attract prosperity in every situation.
- I am a money magnet.
- I am a conduit for wealth and all it brings.
- I am grateful for the abundance that the universe provides.
- My wealth is a reflection of the value I create in the world.
- I am open to receiving wealth from expected and unexpected sources.
- I am aligned with the energy of abundance.
- I am a draw for prosperity.
- I am deserving of all the wealth and cash that comes my way.
- I attract prosperity with every positive thought and action.
- Money comes to me in abundance.
- Wealth will come to me from known and unknown sources.
- I am grateful for the abundance that is constantly flowing into my life.

- I am a beacon of abundance, and it emits from me in all directions.
- I am open to receiving all forms of wealth.
- I attract wealth with my thoughts and actions.
- I am a draw for attracting wealth.
- I will have abundant wealth and prosperity.
- I welcome a life filled with prosperity.
- I will manifest abundance in my life.
- I attract wealth in all its forms.
- I am grateful for the wealth in my life.

CHAPTER 6
AFFIRMATIONS FOR UNSTOPPABLE SUCCESS

- I am the embodiment of black excellence.
- My achievements know no bounds.
- I am a force of brilliance.
- I stand on the shoulders of greatness, paving the way for success.
- I am a trailblazer!
- I am breaking barriers.
- I am a testament to black excellence.
- I am achieving unparalleled success.
- I embrace the legacy of black excellence.
- My success story is already written.
- I am leaving the mark of black excellence in my wake.
- I am a living testament to unshakable determination.

- I rise above challenges.
- I am a vessel of unstoppable success.
- My journey is a celebration of black excellence.
- I am the architect of my success.
- I emit confidence in all I do.
- I emit brilliance in all I do.
- I am a phoenix rising, fueled by flames.
- I emit the essence of black excellence in all I do.
- I am a living testament to the resilience of black excellence.
- I am a living testament to the brilliance of black excellence.
- I am a living testament to the beauty of black excellence.
- I am a force of nature.
- Unstoppable success is my destiny.
- I am creating ripples of success around me.
- I am a manifestation of greatness.
- I am unstoppable.
- Success is not a choice; it is my passion.
- Success guides me forward.
- Success is not a choice; it is my destiny.
- The flames of black excellence fuel my success.

- I navigate the seas of black excellence.
- I am a living testament to the power of black brilliance.
- My success journey is a celebration.
- I am unstoppable because I stand on the shoulders of giants.
- I am a trailblazer, cutting through the darkness with the light.
- I am a manifestation of black brilliance.
- Unstoppable success is my destiny.
- My legacy contributes to the tale of unstoppable success.
- I am a symphony of achievement.
- I orchestrate my own success.
- My success journey is not just personal; it is renowned.
- My success is rooted in the rich soil of black excellence.
- My success is unstoppable.
- There is no hurdle I can not overcome.
- No wall shall burden me to success.
- I will constantly move towards the success I have earned.
- My path to success is already set.
- No obstacle to my success is too high.

CHAPTER 7
AFFIRMATIONS FOR LASER-SHARP FOCUS

- I am a beacon of focus.
- My focus is a powerful force that propels me toward excellence.
- I am unwavering in my concentration.
- Distractions have no power over my focused mind; I am in control.
- I am a laser-focused individual.
- Focus is my superpower.
- I am in the zone where success emerges.
- My concentration is a key that unlocks doors.
- I rise above the chaos, maintaining focus on my goals.
- I am a master of my attention.

- I am a force, tuning out the noise and embracing clarity.
- I am focused and determined to conquer any challenge in my path.
- My focus illuminates my path to black excellence.
- I am unshakeable in my focus.
- I navigate challenges with focused determination, paving the way for success.
- I am drawing in the energy needed for achievement.
- I am centered on the journey to greatness.
- I am grounded on the journey to greatness.
- I am focused on the journey to greatness.
- I am the conductor of my concentration.
- I am an architect of focus.
- Focus is my ally, guiding me through it all.
- I am a visionary.
- I am focused on manifesting my dreams
- My clarity of purpose sets me apart.
- I am in the flow of concentration.
- I embrace the power of aligning my actions with my aspirations.
- I am always accomplishing tasks with precision

- My focus is a beacon of light.
- I rise above challenges with grace and determination
- I am focused and resilient.
- I am achieving excellence effortlessly.
- My focus is a force field that protects my dreams and ambitions.
- I always direct my attention toward the manifestation of my goals.
- I am unswayed by distractions.
- I am unbothered by things off my path.
- Focus is the foundation of my success.
- I nurture my focus with intention
- I am committed to the pursuit of excellence.
- My focus cuts through obstacles and leads me to success.
- I am where distractions fade, and success emerges.
- I am a focused leader, guiding others toward greatness.
- I am the epitome of focus.
- I am a powerhouse of focus.
- I am disciplined.
- I am centered.

- I am focused on manifesting my dreams.
- I am in the flow of focus where success prevails.
- My focus shapes my reality with intention.
- I am a champion of focus.

CHAPTER 8

AFFIRMATIONS FOR DEEP INNER PEACE

- I am a source of calm.
- I choose peace over worry.
- I release any stress with every breath.
- I am a reservoir of inner peace and share it with those around me.
- I embrace stillness. I am the calm.
- I release the need to control everything and trust in the natural flow of life.
- I am grounded.
- I let go of past grievances and open my heart to forgiveness and peace.
- I am centered.
- I am at peace with who I am.
- I choose thoughts and actions that cultivate peace within myself and others.

- I am at peace with the present moments.
- I release the need for perfection and embrace the beauty of imperfection.
- My breath keeps me in a place of inner peace.
- I am a calm and collected individual, even amid chaos.
- I am a peacemaker.
- I am at peace with my past, present, and future.
- I create a space of serenity within my mind.
- I focus on the peace of the present.
- I remove the feeling of doubt in my life.
- I am a vessel of peace.
- I find solace in silence, nurturing my inner peace.
- I am present in the moment, savoring the peace it brings.
- I release tension from my body.
- I am a creator of peace.
- I am a calm and steady force.
- I let go of the need to compare myself to others.
- I find peace in my uniqueness.
- I protect my peace from external influences.
- I am grateful for moments of stillness.

- I am at peace with the ebb and flow of life's natural flow.
- I choose to respond to challenges with a calm and peaceful mind.
- I am a draw for positive energy.
- I bring serenity wherever I go.
- I choose to protect my inner peace.
- I am a source of calm strength.
- I am mindful of my thoughts, choosing those that contribute to inner peace.
- I am a believer in the power of peace.
- I contribute peace and compassion to the world.
- I am at ease with my path and my choices.
- I am centered and composed.
- I let go of the need for constant validation.
- My presence brings peace to those around me.
- I am a reservoir of inner peace, drawing from it in times of need.
- I am peaceful. I choose this over chaos.
- I am a cultivator of inner peace.
- I am at peace with the uncertainties of life.
- I spread peace and its influence wherever I go.

- I am a peaceful soul, contributing to a world that longs for harmony.
- I am grateful for the gift of inner peace.

CHAPTER 9

AFFIRMATIONS FOR FINANCIAL MASTERY

- I am in control of my financial destiny.
- I am making informed and strategic financial decisions.
- I embrace my knowledge of financial literacy.
- My financial goals are clear.
- I attract abundance and prosperity into my life through smart financial choices.
- I am on the path to financial mastery.
- I am debt-free, and I am committed to staying financially liberated.
- Money is a tool for creating the life I desire.
- I am building a solid financial foundation that will support me in the future.

- I am taking actionable steps to achieve financial stability
- I am disciplined in my budgeting.
- My financial goals are clear.
- I am confident in my ability to generate multiple streams of income.
- I am mindful of my spending habits.
- I am grateful for the opportunities to learn more and grow my financial literacy.
- I make decisions that align with my long-term financial goals.
- I am open to exploring and understanding various investment opportunities.
- I am financially literate.
- I attract financial success.
- I am open to receiving wealth from various sources.
- I am resourceful.
- I am building a diverse portfolio that reflects my financial goals and values.
- I am not afraid to take calculated risks for my financial growth.
- I am constantly adapting to the ever-changing financial landscape.
- I am setting short-term and long-term financial goals.

- I love finding creative ways to maximize my financial potential
- I use credit wisely, understanding its impact on my overall finances.
- I make sure that I get the best value for my money.
- I am building a legacy of generational wealth.
- I am a lifelong learner.
- I am confident in my ability to generate wealth.
- I am a doer, creating value and financial success through innovation.
- I welcome the abundance of opportunities that come my way.
- I am a master of prioritizing long-term financial goals.
- I am financially independent.
- I am disciplined and focused on my financial endeavors.
- I am a conscious consumer, making choices that support ethical and sustainable practices.
- I am a responsible borrower, using credit as a tool.

- I am building wealth for myself and my community.
- I am grateful for the financial knowledge I possess.
- I share my financial knowledge with others.
- I am a strategic planner, mapping out my financial goals and the steps to achieve them.
- I am a draw for financial opportunities.
- I am disciplined in my financial habits.
- I am a confident decision-maker when it comes to my finances.
- I am resourceful and resilient, able to navigate financial challenges with grace.
- I am making choices that align with my values and goals.
- I am building a legacy that will benefit generations to come.
- I am grateful for the financial knowledge I gain through every experience.
- I am on a journey of financial mastery, and each step I take brings me closer to my goals.

CHAPTER 10

AFFIRMATIONS FOR STRENGTH AND RESILIENCE

- I am strong.
- I am resilient.
- I embrace challenges as opportunities for growth and transformation.
- I face adversity with courage and emerge stronger.
- I am a survivor, and my resilience knows no bounds.
- I am capable of overcoming any challenge.
- I draw strength from within, tapping into an infinite well of resilience.
- I am like a sturdy tree, bending but not breaking.
- I am resilient in the face of setbacks, using them as stepping stones to success.

- I find strength in every breath I take.
- I am unshakeable in my determination to overcome obstacles.
- I stand strong in the face of life's challenges.
- I bounce back from adversity with resilience and a positive mindset.
- My strength comes from my ability to adapt and learn from every experience.
- I am like a phoenix, rising from the ashes of challenges with renewed strength.
- I have the strength to face whatever comes my way.
- I am a pillar of strength.
- Challenges only make me stronger.
- I welcome challenges as opportunities for growth.
- I draw upon my inner strength to persevere in the face of adversity.
- I am a rock, unyielding in my commitment to overcome challenges.
- I am a beacon of strength, inspiring others with my resilience.
- I rise above challenges.
- I am a survivor.
- I am strong and capable.

- I am a force of nature, resilient in the face of life's storms.
- Challenges are opportunities for me to showcase my strengths.
- I trust in my ability to overcome any obstacle.
- I find strength in adversity.
- My resilience shines in the face of life's trials.
- Each challenge makes me more resilient.
- I am unbreakable. My resilience carries me through tough times.
- I am a source of inspiration, demonstrating strength and resilience to others.
- I trust in my inner strength to carry me through life's challenges.
- I am volatile. I grow stronger with every obstacle I face.
- Challenges are opportunities for me to showcase my inner strength and resilience.
- I am a master of resilience, turning setbacks into comebacks.
- I am a diamond, forged under pressure and shining.
- I am a testament to the challenges I faced.

- My resilience propels me toward a brighter future.
- I am unyielding.
- I am a survivor.
- I am passionate in my commitment to overcome any obstacle in my path.
- I am a source of strength for myself and others -- shining in times of darkness.
- I am a tree with deep roots, grounded in my strength and resilience.
- I rise above challenges with a spirit of determination.
- Challenges may test me, but I beat them with ease.
- I exude the strength and resilience necessary to overcome any obstacle.
- I face challenges with strength and resilience.
- I am capable of overcoming anything life throws at me.

CHAPTER II
AFFIRMATIONS FOR PURPOSE AND PASSION

- I live each day with purpose.
- My passion ignites my soul.
- I am deeply connected to my purpose.
- Every step I take is a purposeful stride toward my dreams and aspirations.
- My passion fuels my creativity.
- I wake up each morning excited, knowing that my purpose propels me forward.
- I express myself authentically in all that I do.
- My passion drives me towards meaningful and fulfilling endeavors.
- I am fully aligned with my life's purpose.

- Passion flows through my veins, infusing my actions with enthusiasm and dedication.
- I am living my ambition with passion.
- My heart beats with the rhythm of my purpose.
- I am passionate about the impact I make.
- I am on a journey of purpose; each step is a testament to my commitment.
- My passion is a powerful force, propelling me towards greatness.
- I am a purpose-driven individual.
- I live with ambition. It permeates every aspect of my life.
- My actions are intentional and impactful.
- Purpose and passion flow effortlessly through me.
- I am attuned to my purpose.
- My passions lead me to a fulfilling life.
- My purpose is the driving force behind my goals, and I pursue them daily.
- I am deeply connected to my passion, and it fuels my enthusiasm for life.
- I align myself with my purpose daily.
- Passion runs through my veins, infusing each moment with vibrancy and zeal.

- I am a purposeful creator.
- My passion is a flame that burns bright.
- I live with purpose, and it brings clarity and direction to my journey.
- I am passionate about contributing to the world.
- My purpose is the force that propels me to make a positive impact.
- I pour my energy into endeavors that fulfill my purpose.
- I wake up every morning with a clear sense of purpose and excitement for the day.
- Determination fuels me, enabling me to overcome any obstacle in my path.
- I am purposeful in my pursuits.
- I am on a journey of purpose.
- My passion is contagious, inspiring others to find and pursue their own purpose.
- My purpose gives me the strength to persevere.
- Every action I take is contributing to the greater good.
- I choose to live authentically.
- I am living my purpose with passion.
- My life is a canvas; my purpose paints it with vibrant and meaningful strokes.

- I am passionate about creating a legacy that reflects my purpose and values.
- My passion guides me through challenges.
- My passion is a source of inner strength.
- I am on a journey of consistency.
- I am committed to learning my purpose.
- I am committed to growing my purpose.
- I am committed to continuously evolving towards my purpose.
- My purpose provides a sense of meaning to my existence.
- I am passionate about being authentically me.

AFFIRMATIONS FOR CHARISMATIC COMMUNICATION

- I communicate with clarity.
- My words foster a sense of connection and understanding.
- I am a confident communicator in all aspects of my life.
- I express myself with authenticity.
- I listen attentively, valuing the perspectives and insights of those around me.
- I am a skilled and effective communicator -- both in written and spoken words.
- My communication builds bridges of harmony and understanding.
- I ensure my message is easily understood.
- My communication allows others to see the real me.

- My words are a powerful tool for building positive relationships with others.
- I engage in open and honest communication.
- I am fostering trust and transparency when I speak to my peers.
- I communicate with empathy.
- I am a confident public speaker, captivating my audience with my words.
- My communication style promotes collaboration and teamwork.
- I am a clear and concise communicator.
- I express myself confidently in both professional and personal settings.
- I am skilled at resolving conflicts through effective communication.
- I choose words that uplift and inspire, creating a positive outlook.
- I am a mindful listener, fully present in the conversations I engage in.
- I communicate with assertiveness, expressing my thoughts and ideas with conviction.
- I strive to eliminate confusion and misunderstanding in my speaking.

- I use humor appropriately to lighten the mood and create a positive atmosphere.
- I am open to feedback and communicate my thoughts with humility.
- I am a respectful communicator, valuing diverse opinions and perspectives.
- My communication is solution-oriented.
- I find common ground and reach agreements amicably.
- I communicate with gratitude.
- I am a clear and effective writer.
- I am a confident conversationalist, engaging in meaningful dialogue with ease.
- I express gratitude through my words.
- I communicate with enthusiasm, infusing my words with passion and energy.
- I am a storyteller, captivating audiences with narratives that inspire.
- I am a storyteller; I resonate with my audience.
- My communication is free from judgment, creating a safe space for open dialogue.
- I present information with poise and clarity.
- I choose words that uplift and encourage, fostering a positive environment.

- I am an effective mediator, facilitating constructive communication between others.
- I communicate with authenticity.
- I am a capable communicator, tailoring my speech to the needs of the situation.
- I express myself assertively and honestly.
- I am a master of written communication.
- I use positive affirmations to enhance my communication skills.
- I communicate with confidence and assurance.
- I am a confident and engaging speaker, capturing the attention of my audience effortlessly.
- My communication style fosters unity among diverse groups.
- I am a master of effective communication.
- I am a clear and concise communicator.
- I am a powerful and influential communicator.
- My words spread warmth and understanding wherever I go.

CHAPTER 13

AFFIRMATIONS FOR MAGNETIZING LOVE AND RELATIONSHIPS

- Our love is a celebration of the beauty found in our shared experiences and mutual understanding.
- In the dance of our love, every step is a joyful celebration of our unique connection.
- We are partners in love, navigating the journey of life with shared dreams and unwavering support.
- Our love is a powerful affirmation of the strength and resilience within our hearts.
- With each passing day, our bond deepens, creating a love that stands the test of time.
- We embrace our differences, knowing they enrich the tapestry of our love story.

- Our connection is a symphony, harmonizing the melodies of respect, passion, and mutual admiration.
- Through the highs and lows, our love remains a steadfast anchor, grounding us in strength.
- In the gallery of our relationship, every moment is a masterpiece painted with the colors of joy and unity.
- Our love is a legacy, a testament to the beauty and power of black hearts entwined.
- With each sunrise, our love is reborn, bringing new opportunities for growth, understanding, and joy.
- We are architects of our love story, building a foundation of trust, communication, and shared laughter.
- Our love is a journey.
- In the garden of our love, we nurture the seeds of trust, passion, and understanding.
- Our love remains unshakeable through challenges.
- We celebrate our individuality within the unity of our love, creating a space for authenticity and growth.

- Our love is a dance: a rhythmic celebration of partnership, resilience, and shared dreams.
- Every embrace is a reminder of the warmth and comfort found in the arms of a love that understands.
- Our love is an affirmation of the beauty within our souls.
- In the tapestry of our relationship, respect is the thread that weaves a pattern of lasting connection.
- Our love is a flame that burns with the intensity of shared dreams, unwavering support, and passion.
- We cultivate a love that blossoms with shared values and dreams.
- Our laughter echoes through the corridors of our relationship, creating a lighthearted bond.
- Our love is a collaboration, each day an opportunity to create a masterpiece painted with shared joy.
- Our love remains a constant, a source of strength and comfort.

- We are partners in growth, encouraging each other to reach new heights in our personal and shared journeys.
- Respect, admiration, and the shared values that bind us together.
- In the symphony of our love, every note is a reflection of the harmonious partnership we've built.
- We appreciate the beauty in our differences.
- Our love is a sanctuary.
- Through challenges, our love remains resilient, a testament to our ability to overcome anything together.
- We are co-authors of a love story that unfolds with each shared moment, creating a narrative of joy and strength.
- We shine brightly with the warmth and understanding that illuminates our path.
- Our love becomes a powerful force, propelling us toward a future of shared success.
- We are a team navigating the journey of life with a love that's built on communication, trust, and admiration.

- Our love is a masterpiece full of compassion, understanding, and shared growth.
- In the tapestry of our relationship, respect and admiration create a pattern of enduring connection.
- We celebrate our shared heritage.
- Our love remains unyielding, a testament to our commitment and understanding.
- Our love story is vibrant and joyous.
- Our love is a melody -- harmonizing the individual notes of our hearts into a beautiful and unique composition.
- We are partners in joy -- creating a space where laughter and shared happiness are abundant.
- Our love is a testament to the beauty within our hearts.
- Our love becomes a roadmap, guiding us toward a future of mutual success and fulfillment.
- We celebrate the journey of our love, recognizing that each step is a precious moment in our shared narrative.

- Our love is a dance, a rhythmic expression of joy, understanding, and the beauty found in our connection.
- This love becomes a collaborative effort, propelling us toward shared success.
- We are architects of our own happiness -- building a foundation of love, trust, and mutual respect.
- In our relationship, each shared experience is a masterpiece.
- Our love remains constant between us.

CHAPTER 14

AFFIRMATIONS FOR GOAL ACHIEVEMENT AND AMBITION

- I am a powerhouse of ambition, setting high goals and surpassing them with dedication and skill.

- Every goal I set is a challenge I embrace, knowing that it pushes me to reach new heights.

- My ambition is the driving force behind my success; I am a relentless achiever, always hungry for more.

- I am not afraid to dream big because I have the skills, determination, and talent to turn my dreams into reality.

- I approach every game with the hunger of a champion, eager to showcase my skills and lead my team to victory.

- My goals are not limits; they are stepping stones to even greater achievements on and off the field.
- I am a high achiever, setting the bar high and shattering expectations with my relentless work ethic.
- I set ambitious goals because I know I have the ability to achieve them.
- I tackle everything with passion and dedication.
- I am goal-oriented.
- Ambition courses through my veins.
- I thrive on challenges because they fuel my ambition and drive me to become the best I can be.
- My goals are not just aspirations; they are promises I make to myself to strive for greatness every day.
- I am not satisfied with mediocrity.
- Each victory is a celebration of my ambition and hard work.
- Each victory is a testament to the dedication I bring to my sport.
- I set ambitious goals because I believe in my ability to overcome any challenge and emerge victorious.

- I understand that setbacks are opportunities to learn and grow even stronger.
- I am a goal crusher who turns obstacles into stepping stones on my journey to greatness.
- My ambition is my secret weapon.
- My ambition gives me the edge I need to outperform and outshine.
- My ambition is a fire within me for my greatness.
- I am not afraid to challenge myself and push beyond my comfort zone.
- Every opportunity is an opportunity to showcase my ambition and determination.
- I am goal-oriented, with a vision for success and the drive to make it happen.
- My goals are like milestones.
- I approach every challenge with the mindset of a champion, fueled by the ambition to outperform and excel.
- Every training is a chance to refine my skills and get closer to my dreams.
- My ambition is my compass, guiding me through the complexities of competition with focus and determination.

- Every goal I set is a challenge I welcome.
- I am a goal-getter, constantly pushing the boundaries of what I can achieve.
- My ambition is a driving force that propels me forward, even when the road ahead seems challenging.
- I set ambitious goals because I know they fuel my passion, determination, and hunger for success.
- Every achievement is a testament to my ambition.
- I am not defined by setbacks.
- My goals are not just dreams; they are visions of the success I am destined to achieve.
- I constantly raise the bar and inspire others to strive for greatness.
- My ambition is a source of inspiration for those around me.
- I am a high achiever who sets and crushes goals.
- I set ambitious goals because I believe in the limitless potential within me to achieve greatness.
- I embrace challenges with the resilience and ambition of a true individual.

- I am laser-focused on my objectives and unwavering in my commitment to success.
- My ambition is my fuel.
- Every moment is an opportunity to showcase my ambition, skill, and passion for the sport I love.
- I am a high-achieving individual, and my goals are the milestones that guide me toward continued success.
- Small gains lead to significant achievements.
- My ambition is a force that propels me forward.
- I know that achieving goals not only benefits me but inspires others to aim higher.
- I promise to give my all and reach for the stars in my athletic journey.
- I raise the bar for what is possible in my career.

CHAPTER 15

AFFIRMATIONS FOR MINDFULNESS AND STRESS REDUCTION

- I am grounded in the present moment, finding peace and tranquility in the now.
- I release tension with each breath, allowing calmness to wash over me.
- My mind is a sanctuary of peace, free from the burdens of unnecessary stress.
- I approach challenges with a clear and focused mind.
- I am the master of my thoughts, and I choose positivity and serenity.
- I release worry and embrace the present with an open heart and mind.
- Each inhale fills me with calm, and each exhale releases tension from my body.

- I cultivate a mindful awareness that brings clarity and calmness to me daily.
- My mind is a haven of tranquility.
- I am in control of my responses to stress.
- I prioritize self-care and give myself the gift of moments of mindful relaxation.
- I release the need for perfection and embrace the beauty of imperfection with grace.
- I am at peace with what I cannot control, focusing my energy on what I can change.
- My thoughts are free and clear.
- I am present in this moment, appreciating the beauty and simplicity of life.
- I am a beacon of calm energy.
- I let go of stress like water off a duck's back.
- I am the embodiment of peace, and I carry this tranquility with me wherever I go.
- I respond to challenges with a mindful approach.
- I am in tune with my body, recognizing signs of stress and responding with self-compassion.
- I release the need to rush.
- My mind is a clear pool of serenity, reflecting the calmness within my soul.

- I give myself permission to take breaks and recharge, nurturing my total prosperity.
- I am mindful of my thoughts.
- I redirect negativity and embrace positivity.
- I create space for stillness in my daily life, allowing peace to flow into every corner of my being.
- I approach challenges with a sense of curiosity, viewing them as opportunities for growth.
- I release the grip of stress, allowing my shoulders to drop and my mind to ease.
- I am a river of calmness.
- I am present in this moment and fully engaged.
- I am a mindful observer of my thoughts, allowing them to come and go without judgment.
- I nurture my mind with positive thoughts.
- I let go of the need for constant busyness, finding joy in moments of stillness.
- My breath is my anchor, grounding me in the present and calming my inner seas.
- I choose to respond to stress with mindful breaths and thoughtful actions.

- I am resilient in the face of challenges, maintaining a calm and collected demeanor.
- I am a mountain of stability, unmoved by the storms of stress that may pass through.
- I am a mindful creator of my reality, shaping a positive and peaceful existence.
- I surrender to the flow of life, trusting that everything unfolds in perfect timing.
- I am aware of the present moment.
- My mind is a tranquil lake, reflecting the beauty of the present moment.
- I release the need for control, trusting that life unfolds as it should.
- I am a source of calm in the midst of chaos.
- I give myself permission to rest and rejuvenate, honoring the importance of self-care.
- I am a vessel of peace.
- I am resilient in the face of stress.
- I anchor myself in the present moment, letting go of worries about the past or future.
- I create space for mindfulness in my daily routine.

- I attract peace and tranquility into my life.
- I am grateful for the gift of mindfulness.

CHAPTER 16

AFFIRMATIONS FOR SPIRITUAL GROWTH AND ENLIGHTENMENT

- I am a spiritual being on a journey of continuous growth and enlightenment.
- Each day, I expand my awareness and deepen my connection to the divine.
- My spiritual path is uniquely mine.
- I am open to the universe's wisdom, allowing it to guide my spiritual journey.
- I trust in the process of spiritual growth, knowing that each challenge is an opportunity for transformation.
- My heart is a wellspring of love and compassion.
- I welcome the insights that lead me to greater understanding.

- I am aligned with the universe's energy and trust in the divine timing of my spiritual evolution.
- I release fear and embrace love as the guiding force in my spiritual journey.
- I am a vessel of divine light.
- My spiritual growth is a journey of self-discovery, and I am becoming more authentic with each step.
- I trust my intuition to guide me toward spiritual enlightenment and self-realization.
- I am attuned to the rhythms of the universe.
- I am a co-creator of my reality.
- I surrender to the wisdom of the universe.
- I am a draw for spiritual abundance.
- Each moment is an opportunity for spiritual awakening, and I embrace the present with gratitude and awareness.
- I am a channel for divine love and light.
- My spiritual practice nourishes my soul and enhances my connection to the divine.
- I am on a path of self-realization.

- I release attachment to outcomes and surrender to the divine plan unfolding in my life.
- I am a student of life, always learning and growing on my spiritual journey.
- I attract experiences that elevate my consciousness.
- I am evolving into a higher state of awareness with each passing day.
- I trust the unfolding of my spiritual journey, knowing that every step leads me closer to enlightenment.
- I am a beacon of light -- radiating love, compassion, and understanding to those I encounter.
- I am a seeker of inner peace.
- I am in harmony with the universe.
- I release judgment and cultivate acceptance, recognizing the divine essence in every being.
- My heart is a compass, leading me towards experiences and connections that serve my spiritual growth.
- I am a vessel for divine healing energy.

- I am aware of the interconnectedness of all things and honor the sacredness of every living being.
- I trust in the divine unfolding of my life.
- My soul is on a journey of expansion, and I welcome the gifts that come with spiritual growth.
- I am a co-creator of the universe.
- I am a reflection of divine love.
- I am grateful for the challenges on my spiritual path.
- My spirit is resilient.
- I am a seeker of inner wisdom.
- I allow my unique gifts to shine in service to the greater good.
- I am in tune with the energies of the earth.
- I am a draw for spiritual insights, attracting wisdom and revelations that contribute to my enlightenment.
- My soul is a tapestry of experiences.
- I am a conscious creator, using the power of my thoughts to shape a reality aligned with my spiritual aspirations.
- I am a bridge between the material and spiritual realms.

- I cultivate compassion, kindness, and forgiveness in all my interactions.
- I am aligned with the divine purpose of my life.
- I allow my inner brilliance to shine forth with confidence and grace.
- I am a vessel for divine guidance, and I trust the subtle whispers of my intuition to lead me on my path.
- I am one with the universe.

CHAPTER 17

AFFIRMATIONS FOR ATTRACTING ABUNDANCE

- Abundance flows effortlessly into my life, and I am open to receiving its blessings.
- I am a draw for prosperity, and I attract wealth in all its forms.
- My thoughts are aligned with abundance.
- Every day, I am growing richer in wealth, love, and joy.
- Abundance is my birthright.
- I am a prosperity draw, attracting success and abundance in all areas of my life.
- Wealth and abundance are drawn to me as I emit positivity and gratitude.
- I am worthy of receiving unlimited abundance.

- The universe is conspiring to bring me wealth.
- I attract abundance effortlessly.
- I am surrounded by the abundance of the universe.
- Prosperity is a mindset.
- Money flows to me easily and abundantly, and I use it wisely to create a fulfilling life.
- My bank account is a reflection of my abundant mindset.
- The more I give, the more I receive; abundance is a cycle of generosity and flow.
- I am aligned with the energy of abundance.
- I emit positive energy, and abundance is drawn to me like a draw.
- I am a vessel of abundance, and it overflows into every area of my life.
- Abundance is my reality.
- I release any scarcity mindset and welcome the boundless abundance that is my birthright.
- I am open to receiving unexpected gifts of abundance from the universe.
- My mind is a fertile ground for prosperity.
- Abundance is a state of being.
- I am worthy of abundance.

- Every step I take is on the path of abundance.
- I will attract opportunities that lead to financial wealth and personal fulfillment.
- I manifest abundance with every thought and action.
- Abundance is my natural state.
- I am grateful for the abundance that is pouring into my life in expected and unexpected ways.
- The universe is abundant.
- I attract wealth, success, and prosperity effortlessly.
- Abundance is a mindset, and I choose to focus on the limitless possibilities that life offers.
- I am open to receiving miracles of abundance.
- I am a vessel of abundance.
- Money is a positive force in my life.
- I attract financial success with every positive vibration.
- My actions are in alignment with my desire for abundance.
- Abundance is my natural state of being.
- I am deserving of wealth.

- My life is filled with prosperity, and I am grateful for the abundance that surrounds me.
- I am a prosperity draw, attracting success, wealth, and happiness into my life.
- Abundance is a river that flows through me.
- I release all limiting beliefs about money and embrace the infinite possibilities of abundance.
- I inhale prosperity with gratitude.
- I am a draw for financial success.
- I am aligned with the energy of abundance.
- Money is a tool for positive change in my life.
- I am a conscious creator, and I manifest prosperity with intention and purpose.
- Abundance is my birthright, and I claim it with confidence and gratitude.
- I share my prosperity with joy and generosity.

CHAPTER 18

AFFIRMATIONS FOR SENSUAL AND FULFILLING RELATIONSHIPS

- Our love is a dance, a sensual rhythm that binds us together in passion and unity.
- Our connection includes a language of love and speaking volumes without words.
- Our relationship is a celebration of the beauty found in our shared experiences.
- We create an intimate bond that fuels the passion in our black love.
- We communicate a story of sensuality and desire that is uniquely ours.
- Our connection is a canvas painted with vibrant colors of passion, understanding, and unwavering support.
- Our love speaks volumes, a testament to the richness of our sensual and fulfilling

bond.

- Every caress is a promise of affection.
- We revel in the beauty of our black love, celebrating the unique magic within our connection.
- Our relationship is a sanctuary of sensuality, where our souls intertwine in a dance of desire and fulfillment.
- Every touch is an affirmation of the deep connection we share.
- We embrace the sensuality of our black love, creating an atmosphere of passion that ignites our spirits.
- Our relationship is a symphony of desire, each note resonating with the harmony of our sensual connection.
- With every shared moment, our love deepens, creating a foundation of fulfillment that sustains us.
- Our black love is a garden of sensuality.
- Our love weaves together sensuality and fulfillment.
- We explore the depths of our desires, creating an intimate bond that transcends the physical.
- Our love is a journey of sensual exploration.

- With each intimate gesture, we express the profound love that exists in the depths of our black connection.
- Our relationship is a sacred space of sensuality.
- We savor the sweetness of our love, indulging in the pleasure that comes from being deeply connected.
- Every moment we share is an opportunity to express the sensuality that defines our black love.
- Our connection is a melody of desire.
- We move with grace and intention, creating a sensual symphony that echoes through time.
- Our black love is a masterpiece painted with strokes of sensuality, fulfillment, and boundless affection.
- We seal our commitment to a love that is sensual, passionate, and deeply fulfilling.
- Our relationship is a sanctuary of intimacy, where we explore the depths of our desires with trust and openness.
- We celebrate the sensuality of our black love, reveling in the pleasure that comes from being fully connected.

- Sensuality includes a glance, a touch, and every whispered word is an expression of the sensuality that defines our connection.
- Our love is a flame that burns brightly with the intensity of passion and fulfillment.
- We create a sacred space for our desires to unfold, fostering an environment where sensuality thrives.
- Every moment of intimacy is a thread that strengthens the fabric of our love.
- Our black love is a celebration.
- With every shared gaze, we communicate a language of desire that transcends the ordinary.
- Our love story is an exploration of sensuality, a journey where every chapter deepens our connection.
- Every intimate moment is a celebration of our sensual bond, a reminder of the profound love we share.
- Let's do this dance of love forever.
- We embrace the sensuality of our black love, creating an environment where passion flourishes.
- Let's find fulfillment in the sweet symphony of our shared desires.

- Our love is a testament to the beauty of black relationships, where sensuality and fulfillment intertwine.
- We are the compass of love.
- Our love is a journey of sensuality, where every step is a revelation of the passion we share.
- In the quiet moments, our love whispers of fulfillment.
- Every shared secret, every stolen kiss, and every tender caress deepen the sensuality of our connection.
- Our relationship is a fusion of passion and fulfillment, a dance that unfolds in the sacred space we create together.
- With every heartbeat, we synchronize our desires, creating a rhythmic dance of sensuality and connection.
- Our desire blooms in the rich soil of our shared experiences.
- We will stand the test of time.
- We will respect, celebrate, and be united intimately until the end of time.
- Sensuality is one of the many keys to our love story.

CHAPTER 19
AFFIRMATIONS FOR SEXUAL CONFIDENCE AND SATISFACTION

- I am confident in my sexuality and embrace the pleasure it brings to my life.
- My body is a source of joy, and I celebrate its capacity for pleasure and satisfaction.
- I am worthy of experiencing deep sexual satisfaction and fulfillment.
- I trust my instincts and communicate my desires with confidence and clarity.
- I am in tune with my own pleasure.
- I emit sexual confidence, attracting positive and satisfying experiences into my life.
- I release any shame or guilt about my sexuality and embrace it with love and acceptance.

- I am deserving of pleasure and satisfaction in my intimate relationships.
- I am open to exploring and discovering new aspects of my sexuality with curiosity and confidence.
- I trust my body's wisdom and respond to its desires with love and respect.
- I honor my boundaries and communicate them assertively to ensure my satisfaction.
- I allow myself to fully experience the pleasure of the present moment.
- I deserve to have fulfilling and satisfying sexual experiences that bring joy to my life.
- My sexuality is a beautiful and natural part of who I am.
- I am a sexually empowered individual.
- I release any inhibitions that hinder my sexual confidence and allow myself to be free in the expression of my desires.
- I am open to receiving and giving pleasure in ways that align with my values and desires.
- I am confident in expressing my needs and wants in my intimate relationships.
- I trust my body's ability to experience pleasure and respond to my desires.

- I am a draw for positive and satisfying sexual experiences.
- I honor the diversity of desires and preferences.
- I release any negative beliefs about my body and fully appreciate its unique beauty and sensuality.
- I am comfortable in my own skin.
- I deserve to be fully satisfied in my intimate relationships.
- I am a sensual being, and I allow myself to experience pleasure without judgment or shame.
- My sexuality is a gift.
- I am open to learning and growing in my sexuality.
- I am in control of my pleasure, and I make choices that align with my authentic desires.
- Sex is a beautiful thing and not something to abuse.
- I trust my intuition in matters of intimacy.
- I am confident in expressing my desires, and I create a space where my partner feels comfortable doing the same.

- I allow the energy of pleasure to flow freely through me.
- I release any fear or anxiety about my sexuality.
- I am open to the exploration of my desires, and I communicate my fantasies with confidence.
- I trust my ability to create a safe and fulfilling sexual experience for myself and my partner.
- I take steps to cultivate a satisfying and joyful sexual life.
- I embrace my sexuality as a natural and positive aspect of my identity.
- I emit confidence in my sexual expression, allowing myself to be fully present in the moment.
- I am open to receiving love and pleasure in all areas of my life.
- My sexuality is a powerful and beautiful force.
- I trust my body's wisdom to guide me towards experiences that bring deep satisfaction.

- I am confident in my ability to express my desires and boundaries with clarity and kindness.
- I am worthy of deep connection and satisfaction in my intimate relationships.
- I attract experiences that bring deep satisfaction and fulfillment.
- I release any past experiences that may have hindered my sexual confidence and move forward with self-love.
- I am in control of my sexual experiences.
- I trust the ebb and flow of my desires, allowing myself to experience pleasure in its many forms.
- I embrace the full spectrum of pleasure and satisfaction available to me.
- My partner and I have a healthy sexual expression.
- My sexual expression opens my creativity.